Fantasy Field Trips

A Weekend with Dinosaurs

Claire Throp

Raintree

Raintree is an imprint of Capstone Global Library Limited, a company incorporated in England and Wales having its registered office at 7 Pilgrim Street, London, EC4V 6LB – Registered company number: 6695582

www.raintreepublishers.co.uk
myorders@raintreepublishers.co.uk

Text © Capstone Global Library Limited 2014
First published in hardback in 2014
The moral rights of the proprietor have been asserted.

Edited by Dan Nunn and Catherine Veitch
Designed by Cynthia Akiyoshi
Picture research by Ruth Blair
Production by Vicki Fitzgerald
Originated by Capstone Global Library Limited
Printed and bound in China

ISBN 978 1 406 27182 9
17 16 15 14 13
10 9 8 7 6 5 4 3 2 1

British Library Cataloguing in Publication Data
A full catalogue record for this book is available from the British Library.

Acknowledgements
We would like to thank the following for permission to reproduce photographs: Shutterstock pp. 5 children (© iofoto), 5 dinosaur (© DM7), 15 (© remik44992), 16 (© EmeCeDesigns), 28 (© AndreAnita), 29 (© Igor Karasi); Superstock pp. 4 (Blend Images), 6, 12, 22, 24 (Stocktrek Images), 7, 8, 9, 10, 13, 14, 15, 18, 20, 21, 23, 25 and title page, 26 (De Agostini), 11 (dieKleinert), 17 (Image Source), 19 (Science Photo Library), 27 (NovaStock).

Cover photograph of a Tyrannosaurus rex produced with permission of iStockphoto (© jianying yin).

Every effort has been made to contact copyright holders of material reproduced in this book. Any omissions will be rectified in subsequent printings if notice is given to the publisher.

All the Internet addresses (URLs) given in this book were valid at the time of going to press. However, due to the dynamic nature of the Internet, some addresses may have changed, or sites may have changed or ceased to exist since publication. While the author and publisher regret any inconvenience this may cause readers, no responsibility for any such changes can be accepted by either the author or the publisher.

Some words are shown in bold, **like this**. You can find out what they mean by looking in the glossary.

Contents

Let's travel back in time!

If you like dinosaurs, then climb into the time machine and buckle up! We are travelling back in time to 230 million years ago. That was when dinosaurs first appeared on Earth.

Don't forget! Some dinosaurs have very big teeth and would be perfectly happy to eat you for breakfast. So get ready to run if you need to!

But when?

Dinosaurs were around for 160 million years. Different types of dinosaurs lived at different times, so it will take a few trips to visit them all!

Pterodactyl

Diplodocus

Jurassic Period

Dinosaurs lived in a time called the **Mesozoic Era**. This time is divided into the **Triassic Period**, the **Jurassic Period** and the **Cretaceous Period**.

Troodon

Cretaceous Period

The Triassic Period

Our first stop is the **Triassic Period**. Dinosaurs began to appear just after an event that destroyed most of life on Earth. Some people think that an **asteroid** may have hit Earth.

Eoraptor was small for a dinosaur. It was only about 1 metre long.

228 million years ago

One of the earliest dinosaurs was Herrerasaurus.

During the **Triassic Period**, dinosaurs such as Plateosaurus and Syntarsus walked the land. Plateosaurus ate plants that were high above the ground by stretching out its long neck.

Watch out for Syntarsus! It was a meat-eater. It could run fast and had long, sharp claws.

The Jurassic Period

What amazing dinosaurs will we discover in the **Jurassic Period**? Earth was very hot and **humid** at this time. Don't forget your suncream and plenty of water!

Dilophosaurus lived in North America and China. It ate other animals.

190–170 million years ago

Did you know?

Barapasaurus's name means "big-legged lizard"!

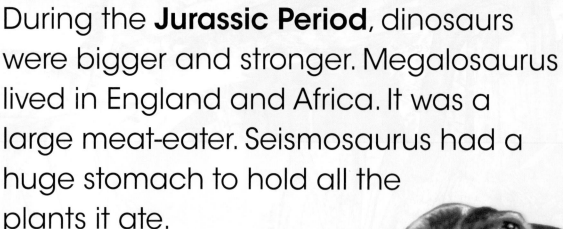

During the **Jurassic Period**, dinosaurs were bigger and stronger. Megalosaurus lived in England and Africa. It was a large meat-eater. Seismosaurus had a huge stomach to hold all the plants it ate.

Megalosaurus

Did you know?

Seismosaurus was about 30 metres in length. That's as long as three buses!

Stegosaurus and Allosaurus lived at a similar time. In fact, Stegosaurus was often part of Allosaurus's dinner! Stegosaurus would have used its tail spikes to protect itself. But it would have been no match for the huge, sharp teeth of Allosaurus.

Stegosaurus

156–135 million years ago

Did you know?

Allosaurus's teeth were 5–10 centimetres long.

If you look out the window of the time machine, you might see creatures flying around. Near the end of the **Jurassic Period**, 147 million years ago, the first flying bird, called Archaeopteryx, appeared.

Did you know?

Archaeopteryx weighed about half a kilogram. That's about the same as 10 bars of chocolate!

147–67 million
years ago

Flying **reptiles** called
Pterosaurs were also swooping
around the skies at this time.

The Cretaceous Period

New dinosaurs began to appear in the **Cretaceous Period**. Protoceratops had a beak-shaped mouth and a frill on its head. It also ate plants.

Protoceratops

Psittacosaurus was so small when it was born that it could almost fit into an adult human's hand!

If you thought that Tyrannosaurus rex was the largest **predator** on land, think again! Spinosaurus was 17 metres long and weighed 20 tonnes. It had a long, narrow head like a crocodile and lived on land and in water.

Spinosaurus

Oviraptor was a small bird-like dinosaur.

Nedoceratops lived in North America and munched on plants. Carcharodontosaurus was a huge meat-eater. It used its large teeth to strike at the neck or side of its **prey**.

Nedoceratops

98–65 million years ago

Carcharodontosaurus lived in North Africa.

Did you know?

The skull of Carcharodontosaurus was as long as 162 centimetres. That's about the height of an average woman.

It is time to find Tyrannosaurus rex. This scary dinosaur lived at the end of the time of the dinosaurs. It had a very good sense of smell, so make sure you have a shower before we go!

Tyrannosaurus rex liked to snack on the plant-eater Edmontosaurus.

Did you know?

Tyrannosaurus rex had teeth that measured up to 15 centimetres long!

The end of the dinosaurs

Phew! What a journey! Sadly, we now have to return home.

Another event on Earth ended the time of the dinosaurs 65 million years ago. Except for birds, almost everything was killed off. **Mammals** were about to rule the world!

Some **fossils** of birds found from the **Cretaceous Period** are similar to pelicans today.

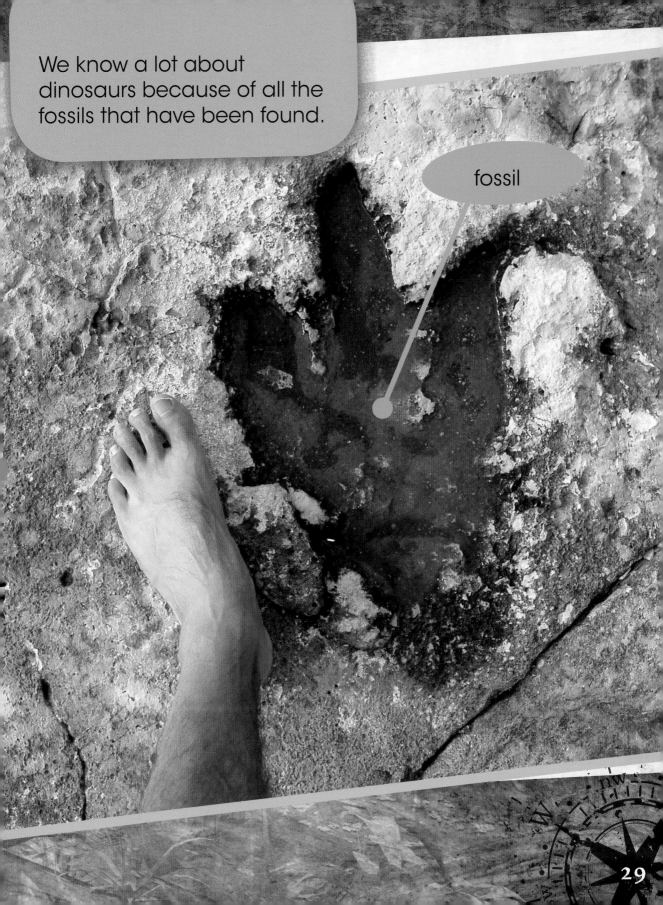

We know a lot about dinosaurs because of all the fossils that have been found.

fossil

Glossary

asteroid large, rocky object that travels around a planet. Some people think an asteroid that hurtled through space and landed on Earth killed most of life on Earth 248 million years ago.

Cretaceous Period about 135 to 63 million years ago

fossil remains of an animal or plant that lived many years ago

humid when there is a lot of water in the air and it feels very hot and sticky

Jurassic Period about 190 to 135 million years ago

mammal warm-blooded animal that is covered in hair or fur. The mother feeds her babies on milk from her own body. For example, cows and humans are mammals.

Mesozoic Era time when dinosaurs lived

predator animal that hunts and eats other animals

prey animal that is eaten by other animals

reptile cold-blooded animal that is often covered in scales. Snakes and lizards are reptiles.

Triassic Period about 230 to 190 million years ago

Find out more

Books

Dinosaur Wars (series), Michael O'Hearn (Raintree, 2011)

Extreme Dinosaurs (series), Rupert Matthews (Raintree, 2012)

First Encyclopedia of Dinosaurs and Prehistoric Life, Sam Taplin (Usborne, 2011)

Websites

learnenglishkids.britishcouncil.org/en/category/ topics/dinosaurs
Try these dinosaur quizzes and games!

www.bbc.co.uk/nature/collections/p00kf6gd
Watch some deadly dinosaur videos on this BBC website.

www.nhm.ac.uk/nature-online/life/dinosaurs-other-extinct-creatures/dino-directory/index.html
Find out everything you could possibly want to know about dinosaurs on the website of the Natural History Museum. Then go and see some of them at the museum itself!

Index